You Think You Zebras

Trace Taylor

Somewhere on the plains of Africa there are zebras...

A zebra uses its ears like sign language to tell others if it is afraid, angry, or comfortable.

Zebras have **ears**.

A zebra can see far away. If you want to see what the world looks like to a zebra, look through a pair of binoculars.

Zebras have **eyes**.

A zebra rubs its nose on the noses of other zebras to warn them that they had better get away.

Zebras have **noses.**

Zebras make barking noises to warn other zebras of danger.

 Zebras have **mouths**.

Zebras inflict vicious, damaging bites on predators that are trying to catch them.

Zebras have **teeth**. 5

A zebra's coat repels most of the heat from the African sun.

 Zebras have **hair**.

A zebra's stripes are unique to each zebra. The stripes confuse the predator's vision, making it hard to catch these striped ponies.

Zebras have **stripes.**

Zebras sleep standing up. They only fall asleep if there are other herd animals like wildebeests or antelope around, keeping a watch for predators.

 Zebras have **legs**.

Zebras kick to defend themselves. Like a kick-boxer, the zebra is so fast that it manages two and even three blows in a row.

Zebras have **hooves.**

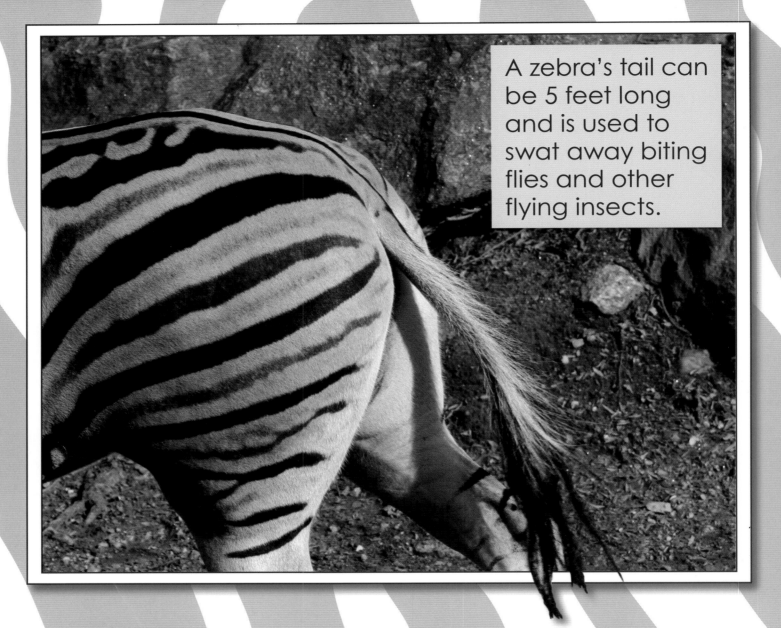

A zebra's tail can be 5 feet long and is used to swat away biting flies and other flying insects.

 10 Zebras have **tails.**

Power Word

have

Where Zebras Live

Africa

Who Lives With the Zebra?

Cheetah

Cheetahs run fast enough to be able to keep up with cars on the highway. They can reach nearly 70 miles per hour in 3 seconds flat. Cheetahs can keep up that speed for the length of 5 football fields. This fast cat wants zebra for dinner.

Crocodile

When zebras go to the water's edge for a drink, or when the herd crosses a river or stream, hungry crocodiles grab the zebras with lightening fast speed and drag them under the water. It's zebra on this toothy predator's grocery list.

Wildebeest

Wildebeest herds prefer to hang out with zebra herds on the open plains. There is safety in numbers. The wildebeests rely on the zebras for early warnings that danger is near. The zebras rely on the wildebeests to stand guard while the zebras sleep.

Hippopotamus

Hippos are considered one of the most dangerous animals in Africa. They bite boats in half. Even crocodiles don't bother these big-mouthed boat-manglers.

Hyena

Hyenas have some of the most powerful jaws in the animal kingdom and have nothing to fear but lions. Zebras had better run when they see a pack of these carnivores on the prowl.

Lions

Lions hunt together. Several lions will hide in the tall grass and wait while the other lions chase the zebra right into their trap.

Leopard

Leopards are excellent tree climbers. When a leopard catches a zebra, it drags it up into a tree. This keeps other predators from stealing the leopard's zebra dinner.

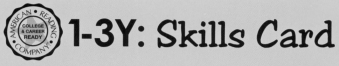

1-3Y: Skills Card

Reader: _____ Room: _____

> "What was this book mainly about?
> How do you know?"

1Y	Listen to and remember the sentence pattern in Yellow books. Use the pattern and pictures to read the rest of the book.
2Y	Point to each word as I read. Use the spaces to separate words.
	Try again if what I say doesn't match the number of words.
3Y	Make the sound of the first letter of the new word on the page, check the picture, then say something that matches both.

I can get my mouth ready for:

b	c	d
f	g	h
j	k	l
m	n	p
r	s	t
v	w	z

1Y: I use the pattern and picture to read each sentence.
2Y: I touch each word as I read.
3Y: I make the sound of the first letter, check the picture, then say something that matches both.

I see a coat.

I see a dollar.

I see a frog.

I see a lady.

I see a puppy.

I see a cup.

I see a crocodile.

I can match the words to the pictures using the first letter sounds.

mouth

legs

tail

nose